Joseph

and His Wonderful Coat

ISBN 978-1-84135-810-9

This edition first published 2010

Published by Award Publications Limited,
The Old Riding School, The Welbeck Estate,
Worksop, Nottinghamshire, S80 3LR

www.awardpublications.co.uk

10 1

Printed in China

First Bible Stories

Joseph
and His Wonderful Coat

by Jackie Andrews
Illustrated by Roger de Klerk

Award Publications Limited

Joseph was Jacob's favourite son, even though
he had eleven others. One day, Jacob gave
Joseph a wonderful new coat, made from all
the colours of the rainbow.

Joseph loved his coat, but his brothers didn't
like it at all!

Most of all, Joseph's brothers hated the way Joseph told them about his dreams. "One day," he said to them, "I will be very great, and you will all bow down to me!"

His brothers were so cross that they decided to teach Joseph a lesson.

They grabbed Joseph, took his new coat from him, and threw him down a dry well. Just then, some traders came by, and the wicked brothers sold Joseph to them to be a slave.

They told their poor father that he had been killed by a wild animal.

Joseph went to work for the man in charge of the King of Egypt's Royal Guard. He worked so well, he was soon put in charge of the other slaves.

Often, they would ask Joseph to explain their dreams for them, and one day the king himself sent for him.

"I have had a very strange dream," said the king. "Can you tell me what it means?"

Joseph told the king his dream meant a very
bad time was coming, when there would not be
enough food for everyone. They had to store as
much food as they could before that happened.

The king was pleased and put Joseph in charge of his foodstore.

When the bad time came, hungry people travelled from all over the land to buy food.
One morning, Joseph was astonished to see all his brothers waiting in line for food. They did not know who he was.

They bowed low to the ground and begged Joseph to sell them some food. While they were loading it into their carts, he secretly hid a silver cup in the bag carried by the youngest.

Joseph's servants stopped them when they tried to leave the city, and found the cup. They brought them all back to Joseph.

"Your brother has stolen from me!" he told them. "You must leave him here to be my slave."

"He didn't take anything, sir!" they cried. "Please don't keep our youngest brother. It would break our father's heart. Take one of us instead!"

Then Joseph told them who he was, and they were amazed and frightened. They had treated him so badly. But Joseph forgave them, and they hugged each other.

They went off joyfully to tell their father the good news, and later, he returned to Egypt with them so he, too, could be with his favourite son again.